Enjoy the walks, and may the sun shine all
day, your boots feel comfortable on your feet
and your pack feels as light as a feather!
Happy walking!
John N. Merrill

Something to ponder.

As we walk around this amazing world, we take for granted the stunning diversity of life and nature. We pass the slopes of mountains and the river valleys. We see birds, insects, animals and all the kaleidoscope of flowers and trees. But let's stop for a moment and just stand in awe of this plethora of sights. However hard we, as humans try, we cannot match the magnificence that our eyes see. Whether you are spiritual or not, you cannot ignore or be moved to wonder at the incredible work of a higher dimension - the divine.

While many would say this is evolution, there still has be "someone", who first thought up the flower, tree, bird, animal, and landscape. You only have to gaze at a small mountain flower and see the delicate stems and petals made to perfection. Whilst the earth's movement have created our landscape, the forces of the divine have been at work to help create that breathtaking view. We on the other-hand have been given eyes and feelings, so that we can appreciate and stand in awe at the sight before us.

So as we wander down a path in woodland or high mountains, where the whole spectrum of life is laid out for us to see. Lets give eternal thanks for being able to walk and see these things first hand. To be able to touch, feel and appreciate the work of the divine, makes the effort more than worthwhile. So, as you walk, stop and ponder at the never ending variety of sights and smells that confront us on each stride we take.

John N. Merrill 2014

WHY I WALK *by Revd. John N. Merrill*

I walk for the exercise; to stretch my legs and muscles; to suck in the fresh air and be free in the wide, wide world, as I walk upon Mother Earth.

I walk to see the trees; that sway in the breeze. To watch the leaves flutter in summer and to walk through on the ground in November. I observe the quietness of winter and watch the buds form ready to emerge when it is their time.

I walk to see the wild flowers; the wood anemones, the blue bells, red campion, and orchids that grow in Spring and early summer.

I walk to listen to the birds that sing in the hedgerows and trees. The friendly Robin is not far away, the started Jay or motionless heron standing at the waters edge. A sudden flash of blue as a kingfisher shoots by.

I walk to see the wild animals; the red fox, the deer, the squirrel and the insects and butterflies, like the dragonfly and red admiral butterfly.

I walk to see the views; to ascend a lofty peak and sit upon the summit surveying everything below, like an eagle high in the air.

I walk for solitude; peace and quiet, to go back to the basics of life, where it is just man and the elements.

I walk in the sunshine, the rain, snow and wind. All has its own beauty and characteristic. All are the cycles of life. I admire the cloudless sky and the rolling clouds of wind and storm.

I walk to see the work of man and God, knowing that we are all connected. Everything has its own beauty.

As the sun sets and I walk home, I know I have lived and experienced a full day, witnessing the whole spectrum of life. I am grateful, very grateful, that God gave me two fine legs, a healthy heart and good lungs to see paradise on Earth.

HOW TO DO A WALK

The walks in this book follow public right of ways, be it a footpath, bridleway, Boat or Rupp. which are marked on the Ordnance Survey 1:25,000 Explorer Series of maps.

On each walk I have detailed which map are needed and I would urge you to carry and use a map. As I walk I always have the map out on the section I am walking, constantly checking that I am walking the right way. Also when coming to any road or path junction, I can check on the map to ensure I take the right route.

Most paths are signed and waymarked with coloured arrows - yellow for footpaths; blue for bridleways - but I would at best describe them as intermittent. They act as confirmation of the right of way you are walking and the arrow usually point in the direction of travel.

The countryside has the added problem of vandalism and you will find path logo's and Information Boards spray painted over and even path signs pointing the wrong way! That is why I always advise carrying the map open on the area you are walking to check you are walking the right way. In my walking instructions I have given the name and number of each main and minor road, canal lock and bridge number, together with house numbers where you turn and the name of the inns passed. Wherever I add what the footpath sign says, plus the stiles, footbridges and kissing gates en route. All to help you have a smooth and trouble free walk.

I confirm that I have walked every route and written what I found at the time of walking.

Most people don't walk correctly with a straight spine and feet parallel to each other, and a few inches apart. Each step starts the cycle of lifting the foot a little way off the ground and placing the heel down first, then moving forward as the foot bends with the toes being last to leave the ground as the cycle begins again. It is all a gentle fluid rolling motion; with practice you can glide across the terrain, effortlessly, for mile after mile.

*I hope you enjoy
these walks and
may I wish you
- Happy Walking!
John N. Merrill*

Companion Walk Guides -

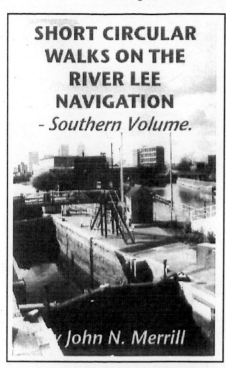

SHORT CIRCULAR WALKS ON THE RIVER LEE NAVIGATION
- Vol 2 - Southern Half.
- 5 walks between Limehouse Basin & Enfield Lock. Plus 28 mile End to End Walk.
The walks also explore the 2012 Olympic Park area.
10 Maps. 38 b/w photos. 68 pages,
£6.95   NEW
ISBN 1-903627-74-5

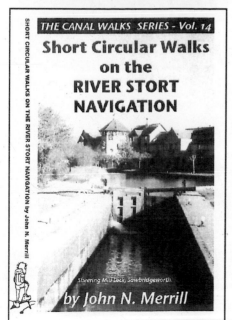

SHORT CIRCULAR WALKS ON THE RIVER STORT NAVIGATION
- 9 walks - 8 short circular 5- 8 miles long and one 18 mile End to End walk.
Considerable history notes and 68 photographs .12 maps. 92 pages. Wire bound
ISBN 1-903627-73-7
£8.95   NEW

U.K. CANAL MUSEUMS -

The London Canal Museum,
12-13, New Wharf Road,
London
N1 9RT
Tel: 020 7713 0836

National Waterways Museum,
Llanthony Warehouse,
Gloucester Docks,
Gloucester,
GL1 2EH
Tel: 01452 318054

The Canal Museum,
Stoke Bruerne,
Towcester,
Northamptonshire
NN12 7SE
Tel: 01604 862229

Foxton Canal Museum,
Middle Lock,
Gumley Road,
Foxton,
Market Harbourough,
Leicestershire
LE17 7RT
Tel: 0116 2792 657

The Boat Museum,
Ellesmere Port,
Cheshire
L65 4FW
Tel: 0151 355 5017

Union Canal Museum,
Manse Road,
Canal Basin,
Linlithgow,
West Lothian,
Scotland
Tel: 01506 671215

The Waterways Museum,
Dutch River Side,
Goole,
East Yorkshire
DN14 5TB
Tel: 01405 768730

Kennet and Avon Canal Museum,
Devizes Wharf,
Couch Lane,
Devizes,
Wiltshire
SN10 1EB
Tel: 01380 729489

Basingstoke Canal Centre,
Mytchett Place Road,
Mytchett,
Surrey
GU16 6DD
Tel: 01252 370073

ABOUT THE WALKS

Whilst every care is taken detailing and describing the walks ikn this book, it should be borne in mind that the countryside changes witgh the seasons and the work of man. I have described the walks to the best of my ability, detailing what I have found actually on the walk in the way of stiles, kissing gates and signs. You should always walk with the appropriate O.S. map as detailed for each walk; open on the walk area for constant reference, or downladed onto your mobile phone. Obviously with the passage of time stiles become broken or replaced by kissing gates; inns change their name or have close down. Signs have a habit of being broken or pushed over and often they are pointing in the wrong direction! All the routes follow public rights of way and only rarely will you find a tree blown down across the path or an electric fence, requiring a small detour. Some rights of way are rerouted such as around a farm but they are generally well signed.

All rights of way have colour coded arrows on marker posts, stiles, gates, path posts, trees and these help you showing the direction of travel.

YELLOW - Public footpath.
BLUE - Public bridleway.
RED - Byway open to all traffic (BOAT).
BLACK - Road used as a public path (RUPP).
WHITE - Concessionary and Permissive path.

The seasons bring occasional problems whilst out walking which should also be borne in mind. In the height of summer the paths become overgrown and you may have to fight your way through in a few places. In low lying areas the fields are full of crops. Usually a defined path leads through. In summer the ground is usually dry but in autumn and winter can be wet and slippery.

The mileage for each walk is based on several calculations -
1. My pedometer reading and steps taken - usually 2,000 to a mile.
2. The route on the map measured.
3. The time I took for the walk - the average person walks at 3mph - 2.5mph uphill.

Allow 20 mins for a mile; 10 mins for 1/2 mile and 5 mins for 1/4 mile.

"For every mile that you walk you extend your life by 21 mins."

Short Circular walks on the River Lee Navigation - Northern Volume.

by Revd. John N. Merrill

THE JOHN MERRILL FOUNDATION
32, Holmesdale, Waltham Cross, Hertfordshire, England. EN8 8QY

Tel/Fax - 01992-762776
E-mail - john@johnmerrillwalkguides.co.uk
www.johnmerrillwalkguides.co.uk
www.thejohnmerrillministry.co.uk
www.londoninterfaithchurch.co.uk

A catalogue record for this book is available from the British Library.

Conceived, edited, typeset and designed by *The John Merrill Foundation*
Printed and handmade by *John N. Merrill.*
Book layout and cover design by *John N. Merrill*

© Text and photographs - by revd. John N. Merrill 2013
© Maps by Revd. John N. Merrill, HonMUniv, R.I.M.A. 2013
© Additional material - Revd. John N. Merrill, HonMUniv, 2013.

ISBN 978 - 1-903627-68-6
First Published - July 2005. Reprinted, enlarged & Revised - July 2013.
Special limited edition.

Typeset in Humanst521 - bold, italic, and plain 11pt, 14pt and 18pt
Main titles in 18pt .**Humanst521 Bd BT** by John Merrill in Adobe Pagemaker on a iMac.

Please note - *The maps in this guide are purely illustrative. You are encouraged to use the appropriate 1:25,000 O.S. Explorer map as detailed on each walk.*

John Merrill confirms he has walked all the routes in this book and detailed what he found. Meticulous research has been undertaken to ensure that this publication is highly accurate at the time of going to press. The publishers, however, cannot be held responsible for alterations, errors, omissions, or for changes in details given. They would welcome information to help keep the book up to date.

Cover design & photo's © The John Merrill Foundation 2013.
Photographs by Revd. John N. Merrill.

The **John Merrill Foundation** maintains the John Merrill Library and archives and administers the worldwide pubishing rights of John Merrill's works in all media formats.

Printed on paper from a 100% sustainable forest.
The John Merrill Foundation plants sufficient trees through the Woodland Trust to replenish the trees used in its publications.

The author outside Chartres Cathedral, France, after walking there from Paris. August 2017.

A little about
Revd. John N. Merrill

John is unique, possessing the skills of a marathon runner, mountain climber and athlete. Since his first 1,000 mile walk through the islands of the Inner and Outer Hebrides in 1970, he has since walked over 219,000 miles and worn out 133 pairs of boots, 49 rucksacks and more than 1,600 pairs of socks. He has brought marathon walking to Olympic standard. He has done a 1,000 mile walk through the Orkneys and Shetlands and a 1,600 mile walk up the length of of the west coast of Ireland. In 1978 he became the first person to walk around the entire coastline of Britain - 7,000 miles. He has walked across Europe, the Alps and Pyrenees - 3,000 miles with 600,000 feet of ascent and descent. In America he has walked the 2,500 mile Appalachian Trail; the Pacific Crest Trail - 2,500 miles in record time; the Continental Divide Trail; became the first person to thru-hike the Buckeye Trail - 1,350 miles in Ohio and completed a unique 4,260 mile walk in 178 days coast to coast across America. He has climbed all the mountains in New Mexico and walked all the trails.

In Britain he has walked all the National Trails many times; linked all the National Parks and trails in a 2,060 mile walk; completed a 1,608 mile Land's End to John o' Groats walk and countless other unique walks. He has walked three times to Santiago de Compostella (Spain) via different routes; to St. Olav's Shrine in Norway - 420 miles; walked to Assisi, St. Gilles du Gard, the Cathar Ways and to Mont St. Michel. He has walked every long distance path in France and Germany, and walked to every pilgrimage destination in England and France, and extensively walked in every country in Europe.

He has walked in Africa; all the trails in the Hong Kong Islands; and completed five trekking expeditions to the Himalyas and India. Not only is he the world's leading marathon walker he is Britain's most experienced walker. John is author of more than 440 walk guides which have sold more than 4 million copies with more than 1 million sold on the Peak District alone. He has created more than 80 challenge walks which have been used to raise, so far, more than a £1 million for different charities.

John has never broken a bone or been lost and never had any trouble anywhere. He still walks in the same body he was born with, has had no replacements and does not use poles. This he puts down to his deep spiritual nature and in 2010 he was ordained as a multi-faith Minister - a universal monk, *"honouring and embracing all faiths and none"*. He conducts weddings and funerals, teaches Qigong and is a Reiki practioner. He gives talks all over the UK.

Contents

INTRODUCTION

I first became aware of the Lee Valley and the River Lee Navigation, when I began planning a walk from London to Walsingham, tracing an old pilgrimage route. I was amazed that such an attractive area lay so close to London and its suburbs and proved to be, as all canals are, a haven in a metropolis. Further impetus was gained with my girlfriend living near Waltham Abbey!

Looking on the map the section of the navigation from Bow to Ponders End was basically devoid of other countryside paths to make circular walks, because of the sprawl of suburbia. I therefore concentrated from Ponders End to the end of the navigation at Hertford. This area provides many varied and delightful short circular walks.

These short ten circular walks explore this area fully and all interlock. Combined they bring you to historical buildings, fine towns and villages and an area rich in wildlife. Step out and enjoy this water filled valley where narrow boats meander.

Some brief history notes -

RIVER LEE NAVIGATION -

Length - Limehouse Basin, Bow to Hertford - 27 3/4 miles.
19 locks.

The River Lee has been, since Roman times, an important trade route to London. An Act of 1571 for an artificial cut was made to help speed up the traffic. At the same time a pound at Waltham Abbey with lock gates - a similar principal to today - was made and is one of the earliest in the country. During the 18th and 19th. century the navigation was improved, these included in 1769 the Waltham, Edmonton and Hackney Cuts (avoiding the River Lee) and pound locks was opened. In 1911 The Lee Conservancy bought the River Stort Navigation and improved it together with the River Lee. By 1930, 130 ton boats could reach Enfield and 100 ton to Ware and Hertford. During the rest of the 20th. century many improvements were made including mechanised locks. Whilst many of the locks vary in size the majority are - 85 ft long by 16 ft wide and between 5 and 7 feet deep. Upto Enfield Lock they are double locks and beyond to Hertford, single locks. The river can be either spelt Lee or Lea.

RIVER SHORT NAVIGATION -

Length - Fieldes weir to Bishop Stortford - 13 3/4 miles
15 locks.

Although more than 200 years old, it has never been commercially viable, and has not been used for transportation for over fifty years. Opened in October 1769, giving Bishop Stortford's malt industry access to the country. The owner was Sir George Duckett who later built the Hertford Union Canal.

THE LEE VALLEY REGIONAL PARK -

The first regional park in Britain, now covering 10,000 acres, along 26 miles of the River Lee (Lea). There are many picnic areas, car parks along its length, with excellent bus and rail links.

Enfield Lock.

River Lee Navigation near Waltham Abbey.

AROUND KING GEORGE'S RESERVOIR - 6 MILES

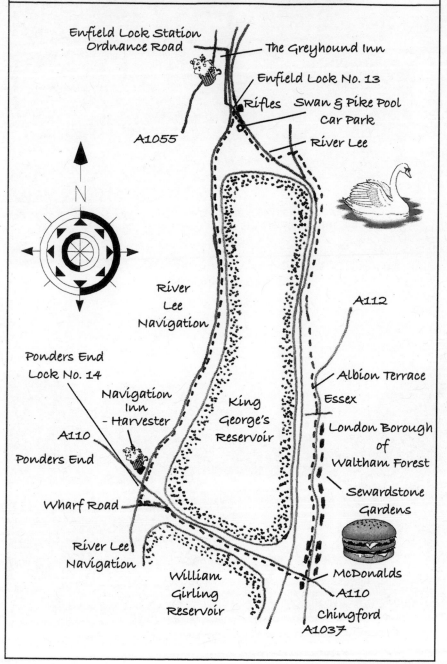

Enfield Lock Station
Ordnance Road

The Greyhound Inn

Enfield Lock No. 13

Rifles   Swan & Pike Pool
Car Park

A1055

River Lee

N

River
Lee
Navigation

A112

Ponders End
Lock No. 14

Albion Terrace

Navigation
Inn
- Harvester

Essex

King
George's
Reservoir

London Borough
of
Waltham Forest

A110
Ponders End

Wharf Road

Sewardstone
Gardens

River Lee
Navigation

William
Girling
Reservoir

McDonalds

A110

Chingford
A1037

AROUND KING GEORGE'S RESERVOIR - 6 MILES (10 km) - (Enfield Lock and Ponders End Lock.)
- allow 2 1/2 hours

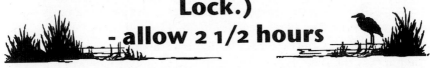

Basic route - Swan & Pike Pool Car Park (Enfield Lock) - Enfield Lock - River Lee - A112 - London Borough of Waltham Forest - A110 crossroads (Chingford) - A110 - Wharf Road - Ponders End Lock No. 14 - River Lee Navigation - Swan & Pike Pool Car Park.
Walked in a clockwise direction.

Map - O.S. 1:25,000 Explorer Series No. 174 - Epping Forest & Lee Valley.

Car Park and start - Swan & Pike Pool, beside the River Lee Navigation, just south of Enfield Lock, reached from the A1055 road. Grid Ref. 372982.

Inns - Navigation Inn, near Ponders End Lock, off Wharf Road and on the opposite side of the River Lee Navigation. The Greyhound Inn at Enfield Lock.

Food - McDonald's Restaurant at the A110/A1037 crossroads (Chingford).

ABOUT THE WALK - The title is a slight misnomer for although you walk around the King George's Reservoir, you only see the earth embankment and not the water! However, don't let this put you off for you first visit Enfield Lock before crossing rivers and following little used paths to the A112. A road walk brings into the London Borough of Waltham Forest to the A112/A110 crossroads Chingford). Here, you turn eastwards along the tree lined reservoir "valley" to Wharf Road and the River Lee Navigation at Ponders End Lock. Heading northwards beside the navigation you return to your start, two miles away.

WALKING INSTRUCTIONS - Exiting the car park, gain the path beside the River Lee Navigation, and turn right; to your left is your return route. Follow the path with the Swan & Pike Pool on your right to the road and Enfield Lock No. 13; this is a single lock. Turn right along the road passing the former Rifles Inn on your left and follow the road back to the car park entrance on the right. Turn left as path signed - Sewardstone. The path keeps the River Lee on your left; keeping ahead past a bridge on your left across it. Continue to a bridge over a side channel and onto another across the river. Follow the path to another bridge over another channel and turn right onto a faint path. This keeps near the river channel on the right to a kissing gate. Continue on the now defined path with the channel on the right and embankment of King George's Reservoir beyond. More than 1/2 mile from the bridge gain a kissing gate and continue ahead for nearly 1/4 mile (5 mins), to where the path turns sharp left with a large black pipe on the opposite bank. In a few yards turn right on a faint path and aim for the far righthand corner of the "field", where there is a wooden stile. Turn left and in 20 yards right to continue along the field boundary (hedge), on your right, to another stile. Keep straight ahead, still the hedge on your right, and onto a kissing gate beside the path sign - Enfield Lock 2.7 km. Here turn right along the A112 road.

Almost immediately pass the row of houses - Albion Terrace - on your right, and soon leave Essex and step into the London Borough of Waltham Forest, the birthplace of William Morris - famed 19th. century poet, designer and socialist. Keep on the pavement for 3/4 mile, past Sewardstone Gardens on the left to the A112/A110 crossroads at Chingford, with McDonald's opposite. Turn right along the A110 - Lee Valley Road - and walk along the tree lined road between the reservoirs for 3/4 mile, to where the road turns right. Cross to your left to Wharf Road - signed Navigation Inn (Beefeater). Pass a small park on the right and in a few yards reach the Lee Valley path and turn right - Enfield Lock, 2 miles. Almost immediately pass Ponders End Lock No. 14, with double locks. Keep on the wide path with the navigation on your left and follow it for nearly two miles back to the Swan & Pike Pool car park on your right.

ENFIELD - The former Rifles Inn reminds us, this area around Enfield Lock was where the famous Lee and Enfield Rifles were made.

THE NAVIGATION INN- Now a Harvester Restaurant, was formerly a Pumping Station.

THE GREYHOUND INN, Enfield Lock - A punt ferry operated here to take workers to the Small Arms Factory.

Swan and Pike Pool.

River Lee.

WALTHAM ABBEY AND ENFIELD LOCK - 6 MILES

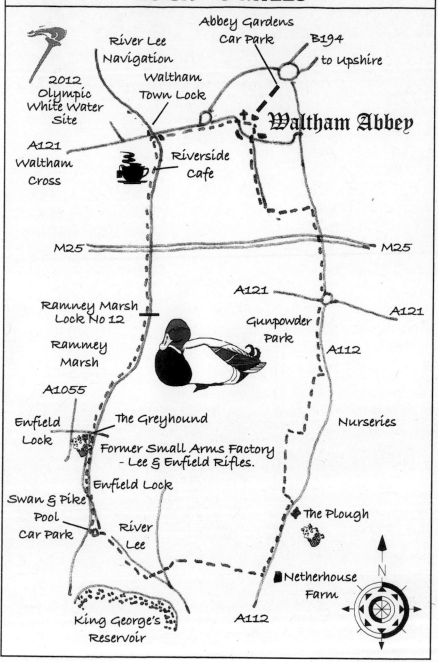

2012 Olympic White Water Site

River Lee Navigation

Abbey Gardens Car Park

B194
to Upshire

Waltham Town Lock

𝔚𝔞𝔩𝔱𝔥𝔞𝔪 𝔄𝔟𝔟𝔢𝔶

A121
Waltham Cross

Riverside Cafe

M25

M25

A121

A121

Ramney Marsh Lock No 12

Gunpowder Park

A121

Rammey Marsh

A112

A1055

Enfield Lock

The Greyhound

Nurseries

Former Small Arms Factory - Lee & Enfield Rifles.

Enfield Lock

Swan & Pike Pool Car Park

River Lee

The Plough

N

Netherhouse Farm

King George's Reservoir

A112

WALTHAM ABBEY AND ENFIELD LOCK
- 6 MILES (10 km.)
- allow 2 1/2 hours.

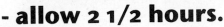

Basic route - Waltham Abbey Gardens Car Park - Waltham Abbey - M25 - A112 - Gunpowder Park - A112 - Netherhouse Farm - Sewardstone Marsh - River Lee - Enfield Lock - River Lee Navigation - M25 - Waltham Town Lock - Waltham Abbey.
Walked in a clockwise direction.

Map - 1:25,000 Explorer Series No. 174 - Epping Forest & Lee Valley.

Car Park and start - Waltham Abbey Gardens Car Park, just off the roundabout at the junction of Harlow, Waltham Abbey and Upshire roads; just off the Greenwich Meridian line at Grid Ref. 383009. Alternative car park at the Swan & Pike Pool, near Enfield Lock.

Inns - Welsh Harp Inn & Green Dragon, Waltham Abbey. The Plough Inn beside the A121. The Greyhound Inn, Enfield Lock.

Teas - Abbey Tea-rooms & Phillots Tea-room, Waltham Abbey. Riverside Cafe, beside the River Lee Navigation, near the A121.

ABOUT THE WALK - A delightful circuit, first through the historic Waltham Abbey. A brief road walk across the M25 brings you to Gunpowder Park and a little used path to Sewardstone. Here picking a small section of the London Loop, you cross Sewardstone Marsh to the River Lee and onto the River Lee Navigation. The final two miles are beside the Navigation to near the Waltham Town Lock and back into Waltham Abbey. You can join this walk with the King George's Reservoir walk to make an 11 mile (18 km.) walk!

WALKING INSTRUCTIONS - Starting from the Waltham Abbey Gardens Car Park, turn right along the path to the former Bloomsbury Forge, on the right, and turn left through the gardens and onto Waltham Abbey. Keep to the lefthand side of it to reach Waltham Abbey Market Place, beside The Welsh Harp Inn. Bear right to the main road and go straight across to walk along Sewardstone Street. Pass the Salvation Army Chapel on the right. Keep ahead into Brooker Street with a road barrier. At the end beside A Plant unit on the left, turn left along the road and where it turns sharp left, keep straight ahead on a fenced path. This brings you to a road and cemetery.

Turn right and follow the road over the M25 to a roundabout of the A121/A112. Go straight across on the Sewardstone Road (A112). Follow the path on its righthand side and pass the entrance to Gunpowder Park on the right. Shortly after and as path signed turn right; this path is little used. First keep to the righthand side of the field, then left along its hedged boundary to its end. Turn right, as path arrowed, and keep the hedge on your left to a path sign. Turn left now on a more defined path, with the hedge on your right and follow it to a wide path. Turn left along it to the A121 road, opposite The Plough Inn. Turn right and follow the road past nurseries on your left to Netherhouse Farm on your left. Turn right along Godwin Close, signed London Loop. Follow the road to a kissing gate keep ahead before turning left then right to follow a grass track way, signed Enfield Lock Station 2.5 km. You cross Sewardstone Marsh and gaining a cross path turn left to a kissing gate and right to a metal footbridge over the River Lee. Continue to another bridge and follow the path right beside the river on your right. Cross another bridge and keep the river on your right to a road end and the Swan & Pike Pool Car park on the left. Turn left through the car park to the River Lee Navigation. Turn right and soon gain the road near the former Rifles Inn and Enfield Lock.

Turn left then right to pass the lock and for the next couple of miles keep the navigation on your right. Pass Rammey Marsh on your left and lock and pass under the M25. 1/4 mile later cross a bridge over the entrance to Hazelmere Marina. Just after is the Riverside Cafe on the left. Continue beside the navigation, on the road, and ascend to the Waltham Cross/Waltham Abbey road; just ahead is Waltham Town Lock. Turn right along the road and keep straight ahead along Highbridge Street to pass the

Tourist Office, cafe and reach Waltham Abbey, which is well worth a visit. Just before the abbey turn left to a former waterwheel and onto the Abbey Gatehouse (14th. century) on the right. Walk through and keep straight ahead on the path back to the Abbey Gardens Car Park, as you do so on your left is a wooden carving of a monk, carved from an oak from Epping Forest. To your right is the site of the cloisters.

WALTHAM ABBEY - Dedicated to the Holy Cross. This fine building was once one of England's largest monasteries. Outside the walls can be seen the resting place of King Harold, killed at the Battle of Hastings in 1066, who built the shrine in 1060. Inside are remarkable circular Norman pillars, some fine stained glass windows and much more; well worth exploring.

GUNPOWDER PARK - Former Royal Ordnance Testing area. The park has been created into a 90 hectare green space, officially opened on June 3rd. 2004.

King Harold's Statue,
Waltham Abbey.

Waltham Abbey, dedicated to the Holy Cross.

Waltham Abbey interior, showing the circular Norman pillars.

WALTHAM ABBEY AND FISHERS GREEN - 4 1/2 MILES

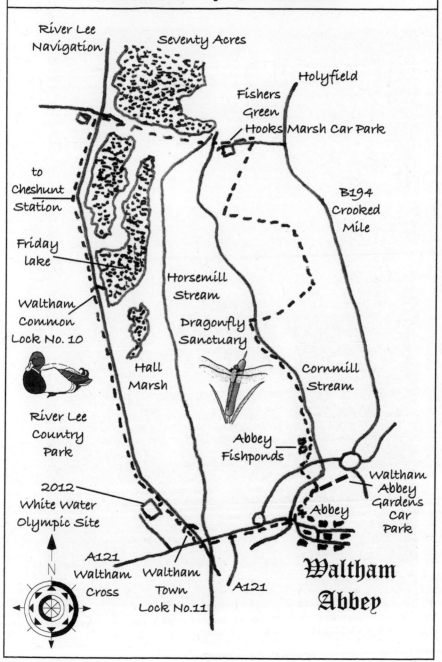

River Lee Navigation

Seventy Acres

Holyfield

Fishers Green

Hooks Marsh Car Park

to Cheshunt Station

B194 Crooked Mile

Friday lake

Horsemill Stream

Waltham Common Lock No. 10

Dragonfly Sanctuary

Hall Marsh

Cornmill Stream

River Lee Country Park

Abbey Fishponds

Waltham Abbey Gardens Car Park

2012 White Water Olympic Site

Abbey

A121 Waltham Cross

Waltham Town Lock No.11

A121

𝔚altham 𝔄bbey

N

WALTHAM ABBEY
AND FISHERS GREEN
- 4 1/2 MILES (7 Km)
- allow 2 hours

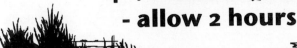

Basic route - Waltham Abbey Gardens Car Park - River Lee Navigation - Waltham Town Lock No. 11 - Waltham Common Lock No. 10 - Seventy Acres - Fishers Green & Hooks Marsh Car Park - Cornmill Stream - Dragonfly Sanctuary - Abbey Fish Ponds - Waltham Abbey - A121 - River Lee Navigation - Waltham Town Lock No. 11 - Waltham Abbey Gardens Car Park.
Walked clockwise.

Map - 1:25,000 Explorer Series No. 174 - Epping Forest & Lee Valley.

Car Park and start - Waltham Abbey Gardens Car Park, just off the roundabout at the junction of Harlow, Waltham Abbey and Upshire roads; just off the Greenwich Meridian Line at Grid Ref. 383009. Other car parks - 1. near Cheshunt Station, Grid Ref. 369023. 2. Hooks Marsh, Grid Ref. 378026.

Inns - several in Waltham Abbey centre - The Welsh Harp Inn & Green Gragon Inn.

Cafe - several in Waltham Abbey centre. Passed en route - Abbey Cornmill Tea-room, beside the Tourist Office.

ABOUT THE WALK - A delightful canal and river walk with much to see on the way. First you follow the River Lee Navigation northwards past a lock and seeing mallards, coots, canada geese and swans. After two miles you cross the navigation and walk between lakes to Hooks Marsh, Fishers Green. Here you turn southwards following a well defined path to the Dragonfly Sanctuary and on beside the Cornmill Stream to Waltham Abbey. The abbey is well worth a visit to see King Harold's Grave and inside the large Norman pillars of this once powerful abbey - you pass the clearly defined Abbey Fish Ponds as you near the abbey at the end.

WALKING INSTRUCTIONS - Starting from the Abbey Gardens Car Park, turn right along the path and left into the Abbey Gardens. Keep ahead to reach the Abbey and bear right beside it to the Tourist Office and Highbridge Street. Keep ahead along this road and then ahead along the Waltham Cross road, passing Macdonalds. Cross the road to the righthand side and pass the Royal Gunpowder Mills entrance. Soon afterwards cross Horsemill Stream and River Lee Navigation. Turn right, as path signed, to the River Lee Navigation and Country Park. Keep ahead past the Waltham Town Lock No. 11. and in nearly a mile pass Waltham Common Lock No. 10. Opposite is Hall Marsh and Friday Lake. Continue beside the navigation and in 1/2 mile pass the Cheshunt Junction car park and sailing club on your left. Here the navigation bears right and in less than a mile approach your first canal bridge. Leave the navigation here, as signed - Fishers Green - and cross the bridge, following a tarmaced track. Follow it straight ahead between the lakes, with Seventy Acres on your left. Cross a metal railed bridge and soon another into Hooks Marsh car park. Continue on the car park road across another bridge over the Horsemill Stream Flood channel and past the Fishers Green Sluice. Soon afterwards pass Fishers Green Farm (historical building) on your left and just after Fishers Green Cottage.

Opposite the cottage turn right, as path signed, over a stile. The well defined path keeps to the righthand side of the field (hedge). Follow it for more than 1/4 mile, before following the path left across the field to a fence. Here as path signed - Cornmill Meadows, keep the fence on your right. Go through a kissing gate and now back in the Lee Valley Country Park, continue ahead beside the fence. Follow the path - grass pathway - right, still by the fence on the right, with tall fir trees on your left. At the end reach the Cornmill Stream and footbridge. Crossover into the Dragonfly Sanctuary and turn left. Keep the mill stream on your left and in 1/2 mile with the Cornmill Meadows on your right, pass the well defined Abbey Fishponds on your right, with the tower of Waltham Abbey ahead. Nearing Waltham Abbey bypass, reach a kissing gate and turn right and soon left to walk through an under pass. Keep ahead over a bridge over the Cornmill Stream, into the Abbey grounds. Reaching a path junction with a building on your left, to your right are the remains of the 14th. century Abbey Gatehouse. Turn left to reach the Abbey Gardens car park. On the right a wooden carved monk - Ancestor by Helena Stylianides. - carved from an oak from Epping Forest.

Waltham Common Lock No. 10

WHARF ROAD AND HOOK'S MARSH - 4 MILES

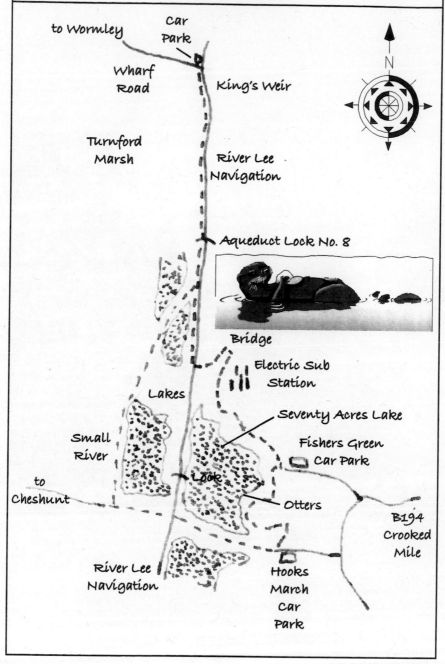

to Wormley

Car Park

Wharf Road

King's Weir

Turnford Marsh

River Lee Navigation

Aqueduct Lock No. 8

Bridge

Electric Sub Station

Lakes

Seventy Acres Lake

Small River

Fishers Green Car Park

to Cheshunt

Lock

Otters

B194 Crooked Mile

River Lee Navigation

Hooks March Car Park

N

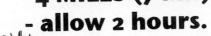

WHARF ROAD
AND HOOK'S MARSH
- 4 MILES (7 km)
- allow 2 hours.

Basic route - Wharf Road Car park - River Lee Navigation - Aqueduct Lock No. 8 - Electric Sub Station - Fishers Green Car Park - Seventy Acres Lake - Otters Area - Hooks Marsh Car Park - River Lee Navigation - Small River - River Lee Navigation - Aqueduct Lock No. 8 - Wharf Road Car Park.
Walked in a clockwise direction.

Map - O.S. 1:25,000 Explorer Series No. 174 - Epping Forest & Lee Valley.

Car park and start - Wharf Road, reached from the A1170 in Wormley. Grid Ref. 372054. Alternative car parks at Fishers Green and Hooks Marsh, reached from the Crooked Mile - Nazeing/Harlow Road.

Refreshments - None; carry what you need. Many nice picnic places passed on the walk.

ABOUT THE WALK - The whole walk is beside water, first along the River Lee Navigation and then beside lakes to Fishers Green and Hooks Marsh. Before the later you pass an area where Otters can be seen. You return past more lakes back to the River Lee Navigation and onto Wharf Road car park.

WALKING INSTRUCTIONS - From Wharf Road car park gain the River Lee Navigation and turn right. Keep the navigation on your left and in about 3/4 mile pass Aqueduct Lock No. 8. 1/4 mile later (5 mins), pass a path sign on the right - Waltham Abbey 4.5 km. - you will be returning on this path later. Little over 1/4 mile later, and before a bridge with a sign - Cheshunt Pits - on the right, turn right then left over the bridge. Follow the wide path down to a sign Fishers Green 1.8 km. Turn left and soon right over a bridge, following the wide path past a large Electric Sub Station on your left. Follow the path to a kissing gate and keep right on the pathway and cross a bridge before reaching Fishers Green car park.

In a few yards bear right, marked Otters, and follow the path to a metal bridge. Cross and turn left - the path sign states Waltham Abbey 3 km. Follow the path past the Otter's Notice board, and follow the curving path to Hooks Marsh Car park. Turn right and cross bridges and then along the path between the lakes and then over a bridge over the River Lee Navigation. Keep straight ahead along the wide trackway and before a bridge with a railway crossing ahead, turn right onto a path beside a lake. Keep the Small River on your left. Ignore all side turnings, keeping straight ahead at all junctions. In more than 1/2 mile now on a smaller path you walk between more lakes; former gravel and sand pits, and a mile from the railway crossing reach the River Lee Navigation beside the sign you passed earlier - Waltham Abbey 4.5 km. Turn left keeping the navigation on your right. Pass Aqueduct Lock No. 8. Little over 1/2 mile later (10 mins), pass King's Weir on your right - reached via the bridge - and just after turn left into the picnic area and cross it back to the car park at the end of Wharf Road.

King's Weir.

Follow the Countryside Code.

* Be safe - plan ahead
and follow any signs.

* Leave gates and property
as you find them.

* Protect plants and animals,
and take your litter home.

* Keep dogs
under close control.

* Consider
other people.

RIVER LEE NAVIGATION
AND KING'S WEIR - 4 MILES

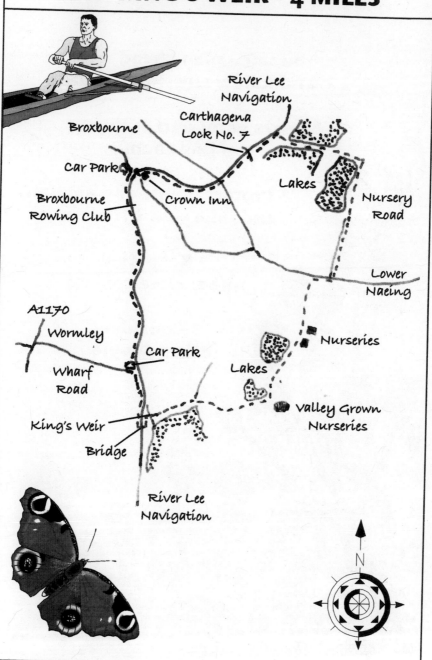

River Lee
Navigation

Carthagena
Lock No. 7

Broxbourne

Car Park

Broxbourne
Rowing Club

Crown Inn

Lakes

Nursery
Road

Lower
Naeing

A1170

Wormley

Car Park

Wharf
Road

Lakes

Nurseries

King's Weir

Valley Grown
Nurseries

Bridge

River Lee
Navigation

N

RIVER LEE NAVIGATION, LOWER NAZEING AND KING'S WEIR
- 4 MILES (7 km)
- allow 2 hours.

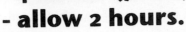

Basic route - Wharf Road Car Park - River Lee Navigation - Broxbourne - Crown Inn - Carthagena Lock No. 7 - Nursery Road - Lower Nazeing - Kiorca Footbridge - King's Weir - River Lee Navigation - Wharf Road Car Park.
Walked clockwise.

Map - 1:25,000 Explorer Series No. 174 - Epping Forest & Lee Valley.

Car Park and start - Wharf Road Car Park, reached from the A1170 in Wormley. Grid Ref. 372054. Alternative car park at at Mill Lane, Broxbourne. Picnic areas at both car parks.

Inn - The Crown Inn, Broxbourne.

Teas - seasonal, just off the route in Mill Lane car park, Broxbourne. Carthagena Lock - snacks and teas.

ABOUT THE WALK - A delightful circuit first along the Navigation, then past lakes to Nursery Road and onto Lower Nazeing. A lane takes you past nurseries before walking past more lakes to the King's Weir and back to the navigation. A short walk along it returns you to the car park.

WALKING INSTRUCTIONS - Gain the River Lee Navigation and turn left. This section of the navigation is a popular rowing section and nearly a mile along it you pass the Broxbourne Rowing Club head quarters on your right. Shortly afterwards pass the side path on your left to Mill Lane car park. Continue by the navigation on the right, across a bridge and onto the road bridge. Cross to your right then left to walk beside the

27

navigation on your left; on the right is the Crown Inn. In more than 1/2 mile pass Carthagena Lock No. 7 - snacks and teas. 120 yards later turn right onto a path signed - Pecks Hill. The defined path leads you between lakes and over a footbridge. Keep straight ahead and bear right at a path junction to continue on a tarmaced path, past another lake on your right to Nursery Road. Turn right as path signed - Nazeing shops 3/4 mile.

Follow the lane to houses, where you turn left then right to continue on a wide path, paralleling Nursery Road to the Lower Nazeing Road. Turn right and in a short distance left onto a tarmaced lane beside Nazeing Antiques on the left. The lane is footpath signed. Pass several nurseries, including Paynes Lane Nurseries and Lakeside Nurseries. As you approach Langridge Cottage and Valley Grown Nurseries, turn right onto a hedged path with a lake on the right. The path later bears right beyond the lake to a track. Go straight across and follow the path to the next lake, and bear right along its edge to a footbridge - Kiorca - across a Flood River Channel. Ascend slightly and keep ahead along the lefthand side of the field on a defined path, which brings you to a wooden causeway beside the King's Weir - similar in design to Dobb's Weir. Reaching the River Lee Navigation, turn left past King's Weir house to a bridge. Cross and turn right to walk beside the navigation on your right. in a 100 yards, bear left on a path and walk through the picnic area on a defined path back to the Wharf Road car park.

Footbridge beside King's Weir.

Dobb's Weir and the Fish & Eels Inn.

BROXBOURNE AND DOBB'S WEIR
- 6 1/2 MILES
AND TWO WALKS OF 4 MILES EACH.

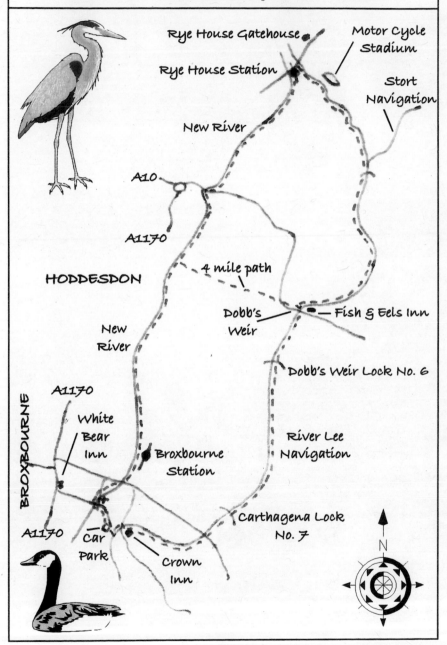

Rye House Gatehouse

Motor Cycle Stadium

Rye House Station

Stort Navigation

New River

A10

A1170

4 mile path

HODDESDON

Dobb's Weir

Fish & Eels Inn

New River

Dobb's Weir Lock No. 6

A1170

BROXBOURNE

White Bear Inn

Broxbourne Station

River Lee Navigation

A1170

Car Park

Crown Inn

Carthagena Lock No. 7

N

BROXBOURNE AND DOBB'S WEIR
- 6 1/2 MILES (11 km.)
- allow 3 hours
Two short circular walks of 4 miles
(7 km.) each
- allow 2 hours each.

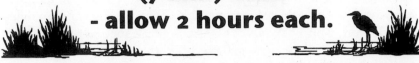

Basic route - Old Mill & Meadows Car park, Broxbourne - River Lee Navigation - The Crown Inn - Carthagena Lock - Dobb's Weir Lock - River Lee Navigation - Fieldes Weir Lock - Rye House Station - New River Path - Broxbourne Station - Old Mill & Meadows Car park, Broxbourne.

Map - O.S. 1:25,000 Explorer Series No. 174 - Epping Forest & Lee Valley.

Car Park and start - Old Mill & Meadows Car park, Broxbourne. Just off Mill Lane near St. Augustine of Canterbury church. Grid Ref. 372068.

For the shorter 4 mile walks you can start from the Dobb's Weir car park. Grid Ref. 385081.

Inns - The Crown, Broxbourne. Fish & Eels, Dobb's Weir. Rye House Inn, Rye House. The Kingfisher, Broxbourne.

Teas - Old & Mill & Meadows Car Park (seasonal). Dobb's Weir car park.

ABOUT THE WALKS - The main route is 6 1/2 miles long, first following the River Lee Navigation from Broxbourne to Rye House. Just off the route here is the historic Rye House Gatehouse, which is well worth a visit. It was built in 1443 from early English brick. From Rye House you return along the banks of the New River. A link path between Dobb's

Weir and Hoddesdon can be used to make two circular walks of nearly 4 miles each - see separate details.

WALKING INSTRUCTIONS - From the car park gain the river path and turn right along it to the River Lee Navigation. Turn left, path signed - Dobb's Weir 2.2 km (1.4 miles). Cross a footbridge and moments later gain the road bridge over the navigation. Cross towards the Crown Inn and turn left to follow the path by the navigation on your left. In 1/2 mile reach Carthagena Lock No. 7. Continue along the path and almost a mile later pass Dobb's Weir Lock No. 6. Continue ahead soon passing the car park and tea room on your right, and ascend to the road, with the Fish & Eels Inn on your right. Turn left then right and cross the causeway across Dobb's Weir and rejoin the navigation on the right. The path to your left is the shorter link path.

Continue beside the navigation on your right and 3/4 mile (15 mins) from Dobb's Weir reach Fieldes Weir Lock No. 5. Just after is the start of the Short Navigation on your right. The final 3/4 mile is a stark contrast to the peaceful canal scene as it brings you past Sainsbury's Distribution Centre on your left and a motor cycle stadium on your right! Just after is the Rye House Inn on the right and here leave the navigation and ascend to the white road bridge. The route now turns left but first it is worthwhile turning right for a short distance to see the Rye House Gatehouse. Retrace your steps back to the bridge and follow the road past Rye House Station. Just after turn left to follow the signed New River Path. The path is well defined, signed and has several kissing gates. Keep the river on your right. In 1/4 mile bear left then right to continue on the path. In a further 1/2 mile cross a road and enter a peaceful section with pine trees. Cross Conduit Lane Bridge East and just after is the path on the left signed Dobb's Weir - the shorter walks link path.

Continue beside the river on the right and on your left is Admiral Walk Lake. Cross a road from Hoddesdon and continue by the river and more than a 1/2 mile later pass Broxbourne Station on your left. Do not descend but keep by the river to a kissing gate, road and the Kingfisher Inn. Turn right and in a few yards turn left to follow the tarmaced path across the green to Church Street and St. Augustine of Canterbury church. Turn left along the street to Mill Lane and turn left then right to regain the car park. On the right is a model railway, open to the public.

LINK PATH - Having crossed Dobb's Weir turn left and follow the path by the river then across the grass to a road and the Lee Valley Caravan Park. Go straight across onto a concrete drive, as path signed. This becomes a track later and leads to a gate and steps to the railway line. Cross with care and continue straight ahead along the edge on the field to a gate and onto the kissing gate beside the New River, path signed Dobb's Weir.

If walking from the New River Path, go through the kissing gate and keep to the lefthand side of the field to a gate and onto the railway line. Cross with care, and continue on a track which becomes a concrete drive, passing the Lee Valley Caravan Park on the right. Gaining the road, go straight across and follow the path by the river to the causeway across Dobb's Weir. Turn right across it or turn left depending on your circuit.

The New River, near Hoddesdon.

RIVER LEE AND STORT
NAVIGATIONS - 6 MILES

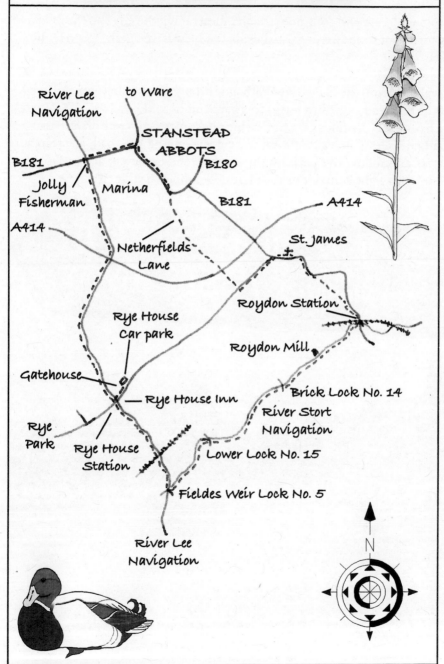

River Lee Navigation

to Ware

STANSTEAD ABBOTS

B181

B180

Jolly Fisherman

Marina

B181

A414

A414

Netherfields Lane

St. James

Roydon Station

Rye House Car park

Roydon Mill

Gatehouse

Rye House Inn

Brick Lock No. 14

River Stort Navigation

Rye Park

Rye House Station

Lower Lock No. 15

Fieldes Weir Lock No. 5

River Lee Navigation

N

RIVERS LEE AND STORT NAVIGATION'S
- 6 MILES (10 km.)
- allow 2 1/2 hours.

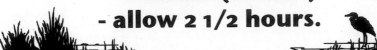

Basic route - Rye House Car park - River Lee Navigation - Jolly Fisherman Inn - Stanstead Abbotts - Netherfield Lane - St. James Church - Roydon Station - River Stort Navigation - Brick Lock No. 14 - Lower Lock No. 15 - Fieldes Weir Lock No. 5 - River Lee Navigation - Rye House Car Park.

Map - O.S. 1:25,000 Explorer Series No. 174 - Epping Forest & Lee Valley.

Car Park and start - Rye House Car park, close of Rye House Gatehouse. Grid Ref. 386099.

Inns - Rye House Inn, Rye House. Jolly Fisherman, Lord Louis Inn and Red Lion Inn in Stanstead Abbots.

ABOUT THE WALK - A walk that explores both the River Lee and River Stort Navigation's. You start from a historic gatehouse and en route pass the historic St. James church, outside Stanstead Abbots. This village has several interesting buildings, including the Abbots House. As you walk beside the River Stort you pass Roydon Mill and two locks. After crossing Fieldes Weir you gain the River Lee Navigation and the final 1/2 mile back to Rye House.

WALKING INSTRUCTIONS - From the car park, close to the gatehouse, turn right out of it to pass Rye House Inn, on your left - this was formerly the Kings Arms Inn and built about 1,600. It was rebuilt in 1980 and has impressive front windows. Just after the inn cross the River Lee Navigation and turn right down to the towpath. Keep straight ahead with the navigation on your right, for the next 1 1/2 miles. After nearly a

35

mile pass under the A414 and 1/4 mile later pass Stanstead Abbotts Marina on the right. Soon after gain the High Street, with the Jolly Fisherman Inn on the left. Turn right into Stanstead Abbotts, passing the Lord Louis Inn and Red Lion Inn on the left - built in 1538. Turn right along Roydon Road, passing a former Cornmill on the right, and soon after the Abbots House. In more than 1/4 mile the road turns left; keep right into Netherfield lane, bridlepath signed - Rye Meads 1 1/2 miles. At first it is a tarred surface but later a track. In 1/4 mile pass the house, Wits End on your right. Later pass a nursery and Ryegate Farm, before walking through a tunnel under the A414. Keep straight ahead on the lefthand side along a fenced path, bridlepath signed.

At the end reach a minor road and turn left to the B181 road. Cross to your right to steps and gate into the graveyard of St. James church. Beside the church, which is open only on Sunday afternoons, during the summer, turn right to regain the road. Turn left following the road right and before the next corner - lefthand - leave the road over a stile and walk diagonally across the field to a footbridge and kissing gate and the B181 road. Turn right and pass Roydon Station and turn right; as you do so you leave Hertfordshire and enter Essex. Follow the road to Roydon Mill with the River Stort Navigation on your right. Before the mill turn left to continue on the towpath with the navigation on your right. 1/4 mile later pass Brick Lock No. 14 with lock keepers cottage dated 1830. Beneath are the letter G and D with a hand in-between. This refers to Sir George Duckett, a onetime owner of the River Stort Navigation. Continue on the towpath and more than 1/2 mile later pass Lower Lock No. 15. 1/2 mile later cross Fieldes Weir and bear left then right to reach Fieldes Lock No. 5 and the River Lee Navigation. Turn right and keep the navigation on your right back to Rye House 3/4 mile away. Pass Sainsbury's Distribution Centre on the left and Rye House Motor Cycle Stadium on the right. Just after gain the white bridge you crossed at the start and turn right past the Rye House Inn and on back to the gatehouse and car park.

RYE HOUSE GATEHOUSE - early brick building, built in 1443, complete with moat. Here the Rye House Plot to kill Charles II and his son James was hatched. However their timing was wrong, for the Royal arrived early and many of the traitors were executed.

ST. JAMES CHURCH, Stanstead Abbots - The nave is 12th century and the tower is 15th century and inside the 18th century interior is unspoilt with box pews and a three decker pulpit. The Baeshe Chapel dates from 1577 and a tomb to the builder, Sir Edward Baeshe, who died in 1587. There are holes in the pews and they are said to spy holes, so the masters could check that their servants were praying properly! St. James is the patron saint of Spain and many pilgrims follow the paths to Santiago de Compostella where his remains are.

Fieldes Weir Lock No. 5

The Rye House Inn.

STANSTEAD ABBOTTS & WARE
- 6 MILES

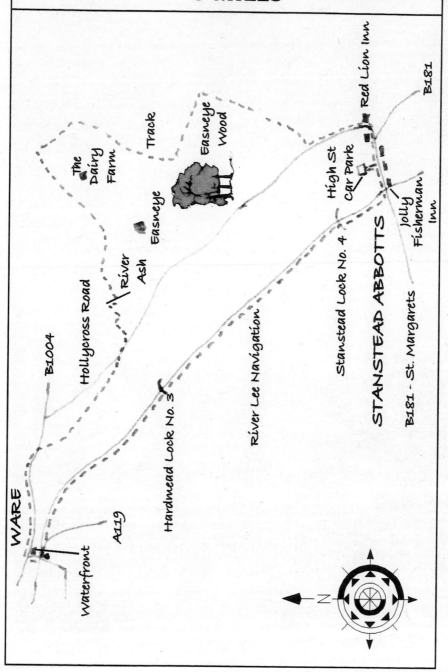

STANSTEAD ABBOTTS AND WARE
- 6 MILES (10 km.)
- allow 2 1/2 hours.

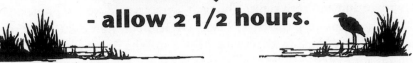

Basic route - Stanstead Abbots - River Lee Navigation - Stanstead Lock No. 4 - Hardmead Lock No. 3 - Ware - Waterfront Inn - Star Street - B1004 - Hollycross Road - River Ash - The Dairy Farm - Easneye Wood - Tracks - Chappel Lane - St. Andrews Church - Clockhouse School - Stanstead Abbots.

Map - O.S. 1:25,000 Explorer Series No. 174 - Epping Forest & Lee Valley.

Car park and start - Stanstead Abbots, High Street Car park, just off the High Street, opposite Abbotts Stove & Cookers, shop.

Inns - Jolly Fisherman, Lord Louis and Red Lion Inn; Stanstead Abbots. Saracens Head, Waterfront, The Victoria, The Angel and others in Ware.

Teas - Stanstead Abbotts and Ware.

ABOUT THE WALK - An almost straight section of the River Lee Navigation, past two locks bring you to the attractive town of Ware. If time permits it is worth a walk along the main street to see many historical buildings and yards, plus The Priory. You return along the otherside of the valley taking a loop around Easneye Wood. As you start to "descend" back to Stanstead Abbotts, you have views to the skyscrapers of London, over twenty miles away. This walk can be joined with the Ware-Hertford walk, making a delightful circuit of more than 12 miles (20 km.); allow 5 hours.

WALKING INSTRUCTIONS - From the car park, just off the High Street in Stanstead Abbotts, return to the High Street and turn right. Follow the road past the shops to the navigation bridge before the Jolly Fisherman Inn and turn right. The path sign states Ware 2 1/4 miles. For the next 50 mins keep the River Lee Navigation on your right. Soon pass Stanstead Lock No. 4, with a swing bridge and the Lee & Short Cruising Club on your right. 3/4 mile later, across the bridge on your right is the Amwell Quarry Nature Reserve (lake) and a picnic area on your left. Continue with the navigation on your right and in more than 1/2 mile reach Hardmead Lock No. 3. Continue by the navigation for almost a mile more past the attractive houses of Ware to the Ware road bridge. Cross the bridge into Ware, with the Saracens Head on your left and the Waterfront Inn on the right. To your left is the main shopping street and well worth exploring.

Immediately after the Waterfront turn right along Star Street - the B1004. Pass The Victoria Inn and later The Angel Inn on the right. Follow the road round to your right and where it starts to ascend on your right is AWA Distribution, a track and path sign. Turn right along here passing allotments on your left. At the end of the track, continue ahead on a path beside the field boundary on your right. Where the hedge turns sharp right, keep left on a defined path to the other side of the field. Keeping along the field edge for a short distance reach steps and path sign before Hollycross Road. Turn right and left almost immediately by a gate bar; path signed. Keep to the lefthand side of the field and soon descend a grass track, then along a level path, curving right to a footbridge on the left. Over bear right to a stile and cross a former railway line to another stile. Turn left along the lefthand side the field, as arrowed, towards the River Ash. Bear right along its banks following the path which curves left, then away from the river to a stile and track to The Dairy Farm up to your right. Follow the track past a house to a junction and turn right. The track takes you through Easneye Wood and curves right. Pass two cottages and then reach a lodge on the right. Here the track turns to Easneye (College).

Keep straight ahead to a gate and continue on a track. In less than 1/4 mile reach a path junction and turn left - Bridle path signed No. 18 - Hunsdon Road 1 mile. 1/4 mile later along the hedged track, with views to your right to London, reach a path crossroads and turn right - Bridle path No. 17 - Stanstead Abbots 1/2 mile. Descend the track and in 1/2 mile reach houses and the Stanstead road. Turn left along Chappel Lane, and

42

pass St. Andrews Church and onto the junction in Stanstead Abbotts with the Clockhouse School on the left. Turn right along the High Street past the Red Lion Inn on the right and part way along turn right back into the car park.

The Clockhouse School.

STANSTEAD ABBOTS - The Clockhouse School dates from the 17th. century. The Red Lion Inn has the date 1538 on the outside. The Lord Louis Inn remembers Lord Mountbatten.

WARE - In 1553, Lady Jane Grey was proclaimed Queen here. Once a major malt industry here, lasted for 600 years until 1994.

WARE AND HERTFORD - 6 MILES

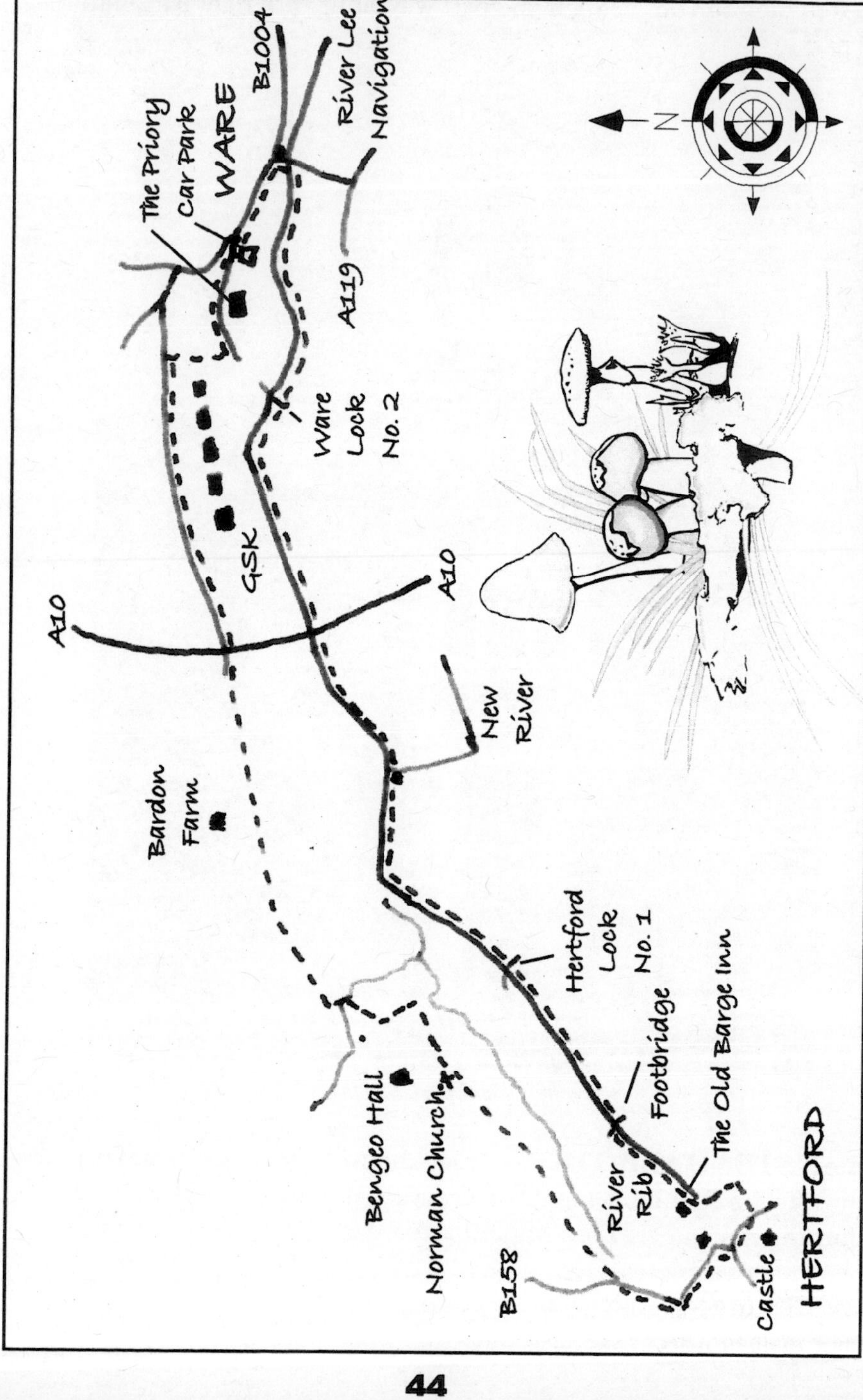

The Priory
Car Park

WARE

B1004

River Lee
Navigation

A119

Ware
Lock
No. 2

GSK

A10

A10

New
River

Bardon
Farm

Hertford
Lock
No. 1

The Old Barge Inn

Footbridge

River Rib

Bengeo Hall

Norman Church

B158

Castle

HERTFORD

WARE AND HERTFORD
- 6 MILES (10 km.)
- allow 2 1/2 hours.

Basic route - Ware - River Lee Navigation - Ware Lock No. 2 - New River - Hertford Lock No. 1 - Central Hertford - Benego Road (B158) - St. Leonard's Norman Church - River Rib - Bardon Farm - A10 - The Chauncy School - GSK Factory - The Priory - Ware.

Map - O.S. 1:25,000 Explorer Series No. 174 - Epping Forest & Lee Valley.

Car park and start - Just off the Main Street, before The Priory.

Inns - Several in Ware, including the Waterfront and Saracens Head. Several in Hertford including The Old Barge and The Woolpack.

Teas - Several in Ware and Hertford. McDonald's in Hertford shopping area.

ABOUT THE WALK - The route explores the final section of the River Lee Navigation, passing its final two locks to Hertford. Before the town you pass the start of the New River. Hertford is worth exploring to see the castle. As you return along the otherside of the valley you pass Hertford's oldest building, the Norman church dedicated to St. Leonard; the Norman apse can clearly be seen. You pass near Benego Hall before walking through woodland near Bardon Farm and across the A10, near a Carmelite Monastery. Entering Ware you pass the GSK complex before descending to Priory Street, passing The Priory. Shortly afterwards you are back on the main street, with the car park off to the right.

WALKING INSTRUCTIONS - From the car park near the western end of the main shopping street (A170), return to the main road and turn right. Pass the shops and inns to the Waterfront Inn and bear right along the main road past the Saracen's Head and turn right onto the River Lee Navigation, path signed Gazebos River Walk. Keep the navigation on your right and in 1/2 mile pass Ware Lock No. 2. In another 1/2 mile pass under the A10. A further 1/2 mile brings you to a building, dated 1856, at the start of the New gauge, New River. Continue with the navigation on your right and in another 1/2 mile pass Hertford Lock No. 1. In another 1/2 mile as you are into Hertford itself, cross a bridge on the right and continue beside the navigation on your left, past moorings areas to the Old Barge Inn on the right. Here the towpath ends. Cross the bridge to your left and into the main shopping area of Hertford. Take the first road on your right - pedestrian shopping area. Pass McDonald's and continue to the main road, with Hertford Castle area beyond.

Turn right over the river and pass the Woolpack Inn and turn right (B158) along Old Cross, passing the Library on the right and some stone remains of St Mary the Less. The church was built in early 1200's and ceased in the 1500's. The remains were found when the Library was built. Continue on the road - Benego road - passing Hertford Brewery on the right; now on Cowbridge. Continue on the main road as it turns right - Port Hill. Here on the left is the house where Capt. W. E. John (1893 - 1968) lived between c1900 - 1912. He is famed for being the author and creator of Biggles. Where the road turns left, beside house no 63, turn right onto a signed path, beside Warren Lodge. Path sign - St. Leonard's Norman Church; Hertford's oldest building. Follow the tarmaced path beside Warren Meadows and in more than 1/2 mile reach the Norman church - opened weekend afternoons during the summer months. Walk through the graveyard to the otherside and turn right, as path signed - Park Road 1/4 mile. First follow the driveway a short distance before turning left through a kissing gate. Follow the path towards a footbridge and the River Rib, but do not cross. Turn left on the defined path by the fence to a stile and footbridge. Cross and bear right on another defined path to a bridge over the river. Behind you in the trees is Benego Hall. Turn left to a road and right along it, path signed - Road as path No. 18 - Park Road 1 mile/Westmill Road 1 1/2 miles.

In a few yards at a bridge turn right onto a fenced path through woodland. Follow the defined path right to pass near Bardon Farm on the left and in-between gardens to a gate. Continue along the righthand side of the fields to more gates to a final one giving access to the track on your left. Turn right and soon pass the turning on your left to the Carmelite Monastery, and cross the A10 bridge. keep straight ahead, passing a lodge on your left, now on a tarmaced road - Park Road. Keep straight ahead and pass the pharmaceutical complex of GSK on the right and Chauncy School on the left. More than 1/2 mile along here and just before the Harrison Bequest cottages, erected AD 1909, turn right down the signed footpath between the GSK multi storey car park, to Priory Street. Turn left and soon pass the The Priory on the right and onto the main road. On your left is St. Mary the Virgin church with the statue of the malters maker in infront. This records the once malt business in Ware which lasted some 600 years. Walk along the main street for a few yards before turning right back into the car park.

HERTFORD - The county seat of the county. The castle - 15th. century gatehouse, is all that remains of a large castle, built to protect London from the Danes. Today the surrounding park and river is a tranquil haven. The **Hertford Museum,** 118, Bull Place, passed on the route, is well worth a visit.

BENGEO HALL - The east front seen from the walk was built in 1745 with two bay windows. The doorway is late 18th. century.

WARE - The Priory was once occupied in the 14th. century by Franciscan .Monks. Founded by Thomas Wake, the Lord of the Manor in 1338. St. Mary the Virgin has a 14th. century octagonal font, and is considered one of the finest in Hertfordshire. The name Chauncy recalls Sir Henry Chauncy who presided over one the last witch trails in England. Jane Wenham was sentenced to death but was reprieved by Queen Anne; this led to the abolishment of witchcraft laws in England. Ware is also famous for "The Great Bed of Ware", which is now in the Victoria and Albert Museum. Dating from the 16th. century it was capable of sleeping twelve people and measures 10 ft. 9 inches square. **Ware Museum ,** 89 High Street, has part of a coverlet for the bed and a WW2 Bunker to explore.

NEW RIVER - Originally built by Sir Hugh Myddleton, a Welsh Engineer, in 1609 -1613, to bring clear water to London. At first it was 40 miles long but today only 23 miles remain and is still used by Thames Water Board; the river being fed mostly by the River Lee, which rises near Luton. Originally the New River was fed by the springs at Chadwell and Amwell, who combined provided a maximum of 10 megalitres a day. A statue in 1738 allowed upto 102 megalitres to be taken from the River Lee. More than century later the amounts were doubled. Today the "river" supplies 38 millions gallons of water to London.

The start of the New River. Building dates from 1856.

The Norman church of St. Leonard, Hertford.

Stanstead Hall, Stanstead Abbotts walk.

Stanstead Lock No. 4.

London Loop Information Board
beside the Swan & Pike Pool near Enfield Lock.

EQUIPMENT NOTES

Today there is a bewildering variety of walking gear, much is superfluous to general walking in Britain. As a basic observation, people over dress for the outdoors. Basically equipment should be serviceable and do the task. I don't use walking poles; humans were built to walk with two legs! The following are some of my thoughts gathered from my walking experiences.

BOOTS - For summer use and day walking I wear lightweight boots. For high mountains and longer trips I prefer a good quality boot with a full leather upper, of medium weight, traditional style ,with a vibram sole. I always add a foam cushioned insole to help cushion the base of my feet.

SOCKS - I generally wear two thick pairs as this helps minimise blisters. The inner pair are of loop stitch variety and approximately 80% wool. The outer are also a thick pair of approximately 80% wool. I often wear double inner socks, which minimise blisters.

CLOTHES & WATERPROOFS - for general walking I wear a T shirt or cotton shirt with a cotton wind jacket on top, and shorts - even in snow! You generate heat as you walk and I prefer to layer my clothes to avoid getting too hot. Depending on the season will dictate how many layers you wear. In soft rain I just use my wind jacket for I know it quickly dries out. In heavy or consistent rain I slip on a poncho, which covers me and my pack and allows air to circulate, while keeping me dry. Only in extreme conditions will I don over-trousers, much preferring to get wet and feel comfortable. I never wear gaiters, except when cross country skiing, or in snow and glacier crossings. I find running shorts and sleeveless T shirts ideal for summer.

FOOD - as I walk I carry bars of chocolate, for they provide instant energy and are light to carry. In winter a flask of hot coffee is welcome. I never carry water and find no hardship from not doing so, but this is a personal matter! From experience I find the more I drink the more I want and sweat. You should always carry some extra food such as trail mix & candy bars etc., for emergencies. Full milk is a very underestimated source of food and liquid.

RUCKSACKS - for day walking I use a rucksack of about 30/40 litre capacity and although it leaves excess space it does mean that the sac is well padded, with an internal frame and padded shoulder straps, chest strap and waist strap. Inside apart from the basics for one day, in winter I carry gloves, wear a hat/cap and carry a spare pullover and a pair of socks.

MAP & COMPASS - when I am walking I always have the relevant map - preferably 1:25,000 scale - open in my hand. This enables me to constantly check that I am walking the right way. In case of bad weather I carry a compass, which once mastered gives you complete confidence in thick cloud or mist - you should always know where you are; I have a built in direction finder! Map reading and compass work is a skill and should be learnt. With modern technology you can now downloaded OS maps to your phone, record your walk, mileage, calories, steps taken, walking speed and time taken.

WALK RECORD CHART

Around King George's Reservoir - 6 miles ....

Waltham Abbey and Enfield Lock - 6 miles ....

Waltham Abbey and Fishers Green - 4 1/2 miles ....

Wharf Road and Hook's Marsh - 4 miles ....

River Lee Navigation and King's Weir - 4 miles ....

Broxbourne and Dobb's Weir - 6 1/2 miles (2 - 4 mile walks) ....

River Lee and Stort Navigations - 6 miles ....

Stanstead Abbotts and Ware - 6 miles ....

Ware and Hertford - 6 miles ....

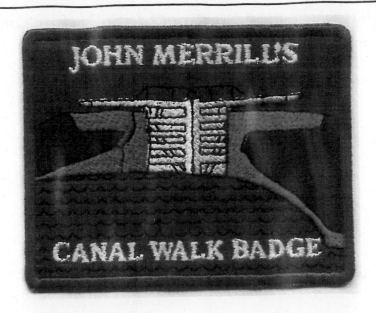

THE JOHN MERRILL CANAL WALK BADGE

Complete FOUR WALKS from this book and get the above special embroidered badge and special signed certificate. Badges are Blue cloth with lettering and lock embroidered in four colours.

BADGE ORDER FORM

Date walks completed..

NAME ....

ADDRESS ....

....

Price: £6.00 each including postage, packing, VAT and signed completion certificate. Amount enclosed (Payable to The John Merrill Foundation) ..
From: THE JOHN MERRILL FOUNDATION,
32, Holmesdale, Waltham Cross, Hertfordshire EN8 8QY
HAPPY WALKING T SHIRT - white & 4 colours - £10.00
e-mail - marathonhiker@aol.com
www.johnmerrillwalkguides.co.uk

*********** *YOU MAY PHOTOCOPY THIS FORM* ***********

OTHER BOOKS by Revd. John N. Merrill

CIRCULAR WALK GUIDES -

SHORT CIRCULAR WALKS IN THE PEAK DISTRICT - Vols. 1 to 9
CIRCULAR WALKS IN WESTERN PEAKLAND
SHORT CIRCULAR WALKS IN THE STAFFORDSHIRE MOORLANDS
SHORT CIRCULAR WALKS - TOWNS & VILLAGES OF THE PEAK DISTRICT
SHORT CIRCULAR WALKS AROUND MATLOCK
SHORT CIRCULAR WALKS IN "PEAK PRACTICE COUNTRY."
SHORT CIRCULAR WALKS IN THE DUKERIES
SHORT CIRCULAR WALKS IN SOUTH YORKSHIRE
SHORT CIRCULAR WALKS IN SOUTH DERBYSHIRE
SHORT CIRCULAR WALKS AROUND BUXTON
SHORT CIRCULAR WALKS AROUND WIRKSWORTH
SHORT CIRCULAR WALKS IN THE HOPE VALLEY
40 SHORT CIRCULAR WALKS IN THE PEAK DISTRICT
CIRCULAR WALKS ON KINDER & BLEAKLOW
SHORT CIRCULAR WALKS IN SOUTH NOTTINGHAMSHIRE
SHORT CIRCULAR WALKS IN CHESHIRE
SHORT CIRCULAR WALKS IN WEST YORKSHIRE
WHITE PEAK DISTRICT AIRCRAFT WRECKS
CIRCULAR WALKS IN THE DERBYSHIRE DALES
SHORT CIRCULAR WALKS FROM BAKEWELL
SHORT CIRCULAR WALKS IN LATHKILL DALE
CIRCULAR WALKS IN THE WHITE PEAK
SHORT CIRCULAR WALKS IN EAST DEVON
SHORT CIRCULAR WALKS AROUND HARROGATE
SHORT CIRCULAR WALKS IN CHARNWOOD FOREST
SHORT CIRCULAR WALKS AROUND CHESTERFIELD
SHORT CIRCULAR WALKS IN THE YORKS DALES - Vol 1 - Southern area.
SHORT CIRCULAR WALKS IN THE AMBER VALLEY (Derbyshire)
SHORT CIRCULAR WALKS IN THE LAKE DISTRICT
SHORT CIRCULAR WALKS IN THE NORTH YORKSHIRE MOORS
SHORT CIRCULAR WALKS IN EAST STAFFORDSHIRE
LONG CIRCULAR WALKS IN THE PEAK DISTRICT - Vol.1 to 5.
DARK PEAK AIRCRAFT WRECK WALKS
LONG CIRCULAR WALKS IN THE STAFFORDSHIRE MOORLANDS
LONG CIRCULAR WALKS IN CHESHIRE
WALKING THE TISSINGTON TRAIL
WALKING THE HIGH PEAK TRAIL
WALKING THE MONSAL TRAIL & SETT VALLEY TRAILS
PEAK DISTRICT WALKING - TEN "TEN MILER'S" - Vol 1 and 2.
CLIMB THE PEAKS OF THE PEAK DISTRICT
PEAK DISTRICT WALK A MONTH Vols One,Two, Three, Four, Five & Six
TRAIN TO WALK Vol. One - The Hope Valley Line
DERBYSHIRE LOST VILLAGE WALKS -Vol One and Two.
CIRCULAR WALKS IN DOVEDALE AND THE MANIFOLD VALLEY
CIRCULAR WALKS AROUND GLOSSOP
WALKING THE LONGDENDALE TRAIL
WALKING THE UPPER DON TRAIL
SHORT CIRCULAR WALKS IN CANNOCK CHASE
CIRCULAR WALKS IN THE DERWENT VALLEY
WALKING THE TRAILS OF NORTH-EAST DERBYSHIRE
WALKING THE PENNINE BRIDLEWAY & CIRCULAR WALKS
SHORT CIRCULAR WALKS ON THE NEW RIVER & SOUTH-EAST HERTFORDSHIRE
SHORT CIRCULAR WALKS IN EPPING FOREST
SHORT CIRCULAR WALKS AROUND SAFFRON WALDEN
LONG CIRCULAR WALKS AROUND HERTFORD
WALKING THE STREETS OF LONDON
LONG CIRCULAR WALKS IN EASTERN HERTFORDSHIRE
LONG CIRCULAR WALKS IN WESTERN HERTFORDSHIRE
WALKS IN THE LONDON BOROUGH OF ENFIELD
WALKS IN THE LONDON BOROUGH OF BARNET
WALKS IN THE LONDON BOROUGH OF HARINGEY
WALK IN THE LONDON BOROUGH OF WALTHAM FOREST
SHORT CIRCULAR WALKS AROUND HERTFORD
THE BIG WALKS OF LONDON
SHORT CIRCULAR WALKS AROUND BISHOP'S STORTFORD
SHORT CIRCULAR WALKS AROUND EPPING DISTRICT
CIRCULAR WALKS IN THE BOROUGH OF BROXBOURNE
LONDON INTERFAITH WALKS - Vol 1 and Vol. 2
LONG CIRCULAR WALKS IN THE NORTH CHILTERNS
SHORT CIRCULAR WALKS IN EASTERN HERTFORDSHIRE
WORCESTERSHIRE VILLAGE WALKS by Des Wright
WARWICKSHIRE VILLAGE WALKS by Des Wright
WALKING AROUND THE ROYAL PARKS OF LONDON
WALKS IN THE LONDON BOROUGH OF CHELSEA AND ROYAL KENSINGTON

CANAL WALKS -

VOL 1 - DERBYSHIRE & NOTTINGHAMSHIRE
VOL 2 - CHESHIRE & STAFFORDSHIRE
VOL 3 - STAFFORDSHIRE
VOL 4 - THE CHESHIRE RING
VOL 5 - THE GRANTHAM CANAL
VOL 6 - SOUTH YORKSHIRE
VOL 7 - THE TRENT & MERSEY CANAL
VOL 8 - WALKING THE DERBY CANAL RING
VOL 9 - WALKING THE LLANGOLLEN CANAL
VOL 10 - CIRCULAR WALKS ON THE CHESTERFIELD CANAL
VOL 11 - CIRCULAR WALKS ON THE CROMFORD CANAL
Vol.13 - SHORT CIRCULAR WALKS ON THE RIVER LEE NAVIGATION -Vol. 1 - North
Vol. 14 - SHORT CIRCULAR WALKS ON THE RIVER STORT NAVIGATION
Vol.15 - SHORT CIRCULAR WALKS ON THE RIVER LEE NAVIGATION - Vol. 2 - South
Vol. 16 - WALKING THE CANALS OF LONDON
Vol 17 - WALKING THE RIVER LEE NAVIGATION
Vol. 20 - SHORT CIRCULAR WALKS IN THE COLNE VALLEY
Vol 21 - THE BLACKWATER & CHELMER NAVIGATION - End to End.
Vol. 22 - NOTTINGHAM'S LOST CANAL by Bernard Chell.
Vol. 23 - WALKING THE RIVER WEY & GODALMING NAVIAGTIONS END TO END
Vol.25 - WALKING THE GRAND UNION CANAL - LONDON TO BIRMINGHAM.

JOHN MERRILL DAY CHALLENGE WALKS

WHITE PEAK CHALLENGE WALK
THE HAPPY HIKER - WHITE PEAK - CHALLENGE WALK
DARK PEAK CHALLENGE WALK
PEAK DISTRICT END TO END WALKS
STAFFORDSHIRE MOORLANDS CHALLENGE WALK

JOHN MERRILL DAY CHALLENGE WALKS

WHITE PEAK CHALLENGE WALK
THE HAPPY HIKER - WHITE PEAK - CHALLENGE WALK No.2
DARK PEAK CHALLENGE WALK
PEAK DISTRICT END TO END WALKS
STAFFORDSHIRE MOORLANDS CHALLENGE WALK
THE LITTLE JOHN CHALLENGE WALK
YORKSHIRE DALES CHALLENGE WALK
NORTH YORKSHIRE MOORS CHALLENGE WALK
LAKELAND CHALLENGE WALK
THE RUTLAND WATER CHALLENGE WALK
MALVERN HILLS CHALLENGE WALK
THE SALTERIS WAY
THE SNOWDON CHALLENGE
CHARNWOOD FOREST CHALLENGE WALK
THREE COUNTIES CHALLENGE WALK (Peak District).
CAL-DER-WENT WALK
THE QUANTOCK WAY
BELVOIR WITCHES CHALLENGE WALK
THE CARNEDDAU CHALLENGE WALK
THE SWEET PEA CHALLENGE WALK
THE LINCOLNSHIRE WOLDS - BLACK DEATH - CHALLENGE WALK
JENNIFER'S CHALLENGE WALK
THE EPPING FOREST CHALLENGE WALK
THE THREE BOROUGH CHALLENGE WALK - NORTH LONDON
THE HERTFORD CHALLENGE WALK
THE BOSHAM CHALLENGE WALK
THE KING JOHN CHALLENGE WALK
THE NORFOLK BROADS CHALLENGE WALK
THE RIVER MIMRAM WALK
THE ISLE OF THANET CHHALENGE WALK
EAST DEVON CHALLENGE WALK

INSTRUCTION & RECORD -

HIKE TO BE FIT.....STROLLING WITH JOHN
THE JOHN MERRILL WALK RECORD BOOK
HIKE THE WORLD - John Merrill's guide to walking & Backpacking.

MULTIPLE DAY WALKS -

THE RIVERS'S WAY
PEAK DISTRICT: HIGH LEVEL ROUTE
PEAK DISTRICT MARATHONS
THE LIMEY WAY
THE PEAKLAND WAY
COMPO'S WAY by Alan Hiley
THE BRIGHTON WAY

COAST WALKS & NATIONAL TRAILS -

ISLE OF WIGHT COAST PATH
PEMBROKESHIRE COAST PATH
THE CLEVELAND WAY
WALKING ANGELSEY'S COASTLINE.
WALKING THE COASTLINE OF THE CHANNEL ISLANDS
THE ISLE OF MAN COASTAL PATH - "The Way of the Gull."
A WALK AROUND HAYLING ISLAND
A WALK AROUND THE ISLE OF SHEPPEY
A WALK AROUND THE ISLE OF JERSEY
WALKING AROUND THE ISLANDS OF ESSEX
WALKING AROUND ESSEX'S COASTLINE - 320 MILES

DERBYSHIRE & PEAK DISTRICT HISTORICAL GUIDES -

A to Z GUIDE OF THE PEAK DISTRICT
DERBYSHIRE INNS - an A to Z guide
HALLS AND CASTLES OF THE PEAK DISTRICT & DERBYSHIRE
TOURING THE PEAK DISTRICT & DERBYSHIRE BY CAR
DERBYSHIRE FOLKLORE
PUNISHMENT IN DERBYSHIRE
CUSTOMS OF THE PEAK DISTRICT & DERBYSHIRE
WINSTER - a souvenir guide
ARKWRIGHT OF CROMFORD
LEGENDS OF DERBYSHIRE
DERBYSHIRE FACTS & RECORDS
TALES FROM THE MINES by Geoffrey Carr
PEAK DISTRICT PLACE NAMES by Martin Spray
DERBYSHIRE THROUGH THE AGES - Vol 1 -DERBYSHIRE IN PREHISTORIC TIMES
SIR JOSEPH PAXTON
FLORENCE NIGHTINGALE
JOHN SMEDLEY
BONNIE PRINCE CHARLIE & 20 mile walk.
THE STORY OF THE EARLS AND DUKES OF DEVONSHIRE

JOHN MERRILL'S MAJOR WALKS -

TURN RIGHT AT LAND'S END
WITH MUSTARD ON MY BACK
TURN RIGHT AT DEATH VALLEY
EMERALD COAST WALK
I CHOSE TO WALK - Why I walk etc.
A WALK IN OHIO - 1,310 miles around the Buckeye Trail.
I AM GUIDED - the story of John's wal;king life.

SKETCH BOOKS -

SKETCHES OF THE PEAK DISTRICT

COLOUR BOOK:-

THE PEAK DISTRICT.......something to remember her by.

OVERSEAS GUIDES -

HIKING IN NEW MEXICO - Vol I - The Sandia and Manzano Mountains.
Vol 2 - Hiking "Billy the Kid" Country.
Vol 4 - N.W. area - " Hiking Indian Country."
"WALKING IN DRACULA COUNTRY" - Romania.
WALKING THE TRAILS OF THE HONG KONG ISLANDS.

VISITOR GUIDES - MATLOCK . BAKEWELL.

ASHBOURNE.

See all my books on -
www.johnmerrillwalkguides.co.uk

Pilgrim Guides -
www.thejohnmerrillministry.co.uk

OTHER LONDON CANAL WALK BOOKS
by JOHN N. MERRILL

SHORT CIRCULAR WALKS ON THE RIVER LEE NAVIGA-TION - Northern Volume - Ponder's End - Hertford.
60 pages, 23 photographs, 10 detailed maps and walks. History notes.
- ISBN 1-903627-68-0 £8.50

SHORT CIRCULAR WALKS ON THE RIVER LEE NAVIGA-TION - Southern Volume - Limehouse basin to Hackney Marsh.
5 walks on the Regent Canal, Hertford Union and Limehouse Cut.
Including Three Mills and its rivers. The guide also details a 28 mile
End to End walk along the Navigation. 68 pages. 10 maps, 30 photographs. ISBN 1-903627-74-5 £8.50

WALK THE RIVER LEE NAVIGATION - Vol One and Two plus
additional walks, in one book. 120 pages. 24 maps. 40 photos.
ISBN 978- £10.95

SHORT CIRCULAR WALKS ON THE RIVER STORT NAVI-GATION
8 circular walks; 1 End to End walk. Full history and photographic
study of this peaceful waterway. 92 pages. 68 photographgs. 12 maps.
ISBN 1-903627- 73-7 £10.95

**SHORT CIRCULAR WALKS ON THE NEW RIVER & SOUTH
EAST HERTFORDSHIRE**
11 walks - 5 to 10 miles long between Waltham Cross and Hertford;
many on the New River. New revised and enlarged edition 68 pages,
24 photographs , 13 detailed maps. History notes.
ISBN 1-903627-69-9   £8.50

WALKING LONDON'S CANALS -
Regent's Canal, River Thames, Isle of Dogs and Grand Union Canal.
10 walks. 108 pages. 85 photos. Wire bound. 14 detailed maps. £9.95
ISBN 978-0-9553691-2-4 £10.95

SHORT CIRCULAR WALKS IN THE COLNE VALLEY
Eight walks on the Grand Union Canal nad Slough Arm, between
Rickmansworth and Uxbridge. 72 pages. 12 maps.
40 photos. ISBN 978-09560649-5-0 £8.50

THE CHEMLER & BACKWATER NAVIGATION - END TO END

MY WALKING PHILOSOPHY
by John N. Merrill

I basically break many of the "accepted" rules of walking, but I believe my technique and approach has brought my walking to a higher level. Walking to me, is not physical fitness but having the right mental approach to the task. All you need is a strong faith. I never consult with anyone or do any research beforehand. All this spoils the experience and "programmes" your mind to what is around the corner. I prefer not to know and discover as I go, this way making a greater impression on me. On a major walk at the end of each day, I run through the next day's stage on the map, so that on setting off the next day I am already programmed as to my day's destination. It is immaterial how far, how much ascent and descent, the day's destination is the key. I do not tick of the miles as I go for this makes the day go slowly and pulls you down mentally. On hills I adopt a steady pace and ascend, never stopping. If you stop on the way this too pulls you down mentally making the ascent seem long. During the day I basically don't stop for anything between 6 and 10 hours, just maintaining a steady comfortable pace. At the end of the day I have still enough energy and determination to carry on. To stop and restart means a couple of miles before I am in the "groove" again.

To many walking the Pennine Way is the ultimate walk, but after reaching Kirk Yetholm with 280 miles walked, you have hardly begun! By the time you have done that distance you have passed through the early stages of adjusting to your new way of life. The rucksack has become more bearable, the blisters have gone and your fitness has soared. But you need to walk 500 miles before you are settled into the task and have comfy feet. After 1,000 miles you are really adjusted and by 1,500 miles you can push yourself relentlessly. By 2,000 miles of continuous walking you are at your peak performance, but after 2,500 miles you are physically declining. You can reach your peak later by doing a reduced daily mileage but by 3,500 miles you are declining and by 4,000 miles I have usually lost 52 pounds in weight and struggling to walk well each day.

I always walk alone, so I can walk at my own pace. If you walk with others on a long walk if their pace is not compatible to yours you are more tired than they at the end of the day. Also you talk a lot which lessens the impact of the scenery and places on the way and you miss seeing the wildlife. I carry no mobile phone nor use poles. I usually wear T shirt and shorts but obviously warmer clothes in mountains and snow. In the pursuit of corporate money, the public are "brain washed" to stay in contact and drink water; they want the sales! I carry no water and don't usually drink during the day for anything upto 8 or ten hours. This is no hardship even when walking across the Mohave desert in 120° F. Once you start to drink you want more and the more you drink the more you sweat. Buddhist monks take this approach and have never come to any harm.My spiritual teaching as a Toaist Buddhist, concurs with their throught and training. You can live for four days without water and forty days without food. An injured walker in the Lake District survived for three weeks in gully, drinking a regular drip of water, until he was eventually found by a rescue party.

Infact US Military studies on thirst, while desert walking, in World War I I found that -

in 80° F heat a man can comfortably walk 45 miles without water.
in 100° F heat, 15 miles
in 120° F heat, 7 miles before collapsing.

Interestingly they found that walking 20 miles in the desert night, they recommended carrying 4 litres of water. During the day this increased to 8 litres.

Walking is the only way to fully appreciate the earth and you see it on its own terms.

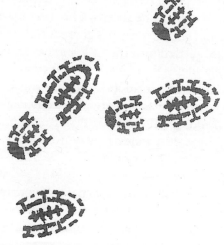

THE PILGRIM'S WAY SERIES by Revd. John N. Merrill

THE WALSINGHAM WAY
- Ely to Walsingham - 72 miles - 1-903627-33-8 ....£8.95
- 56 pages and 40 photographs.

THE WALSINGHAM WAY
- King's Lynn to Walsingham - 35 miles - 1-903627-41 - 9 ....£9.95
- 72 pages and 50 colour photographs.

THE WALSINGHAM WAY - 77 miles - Bury St. Edmunds to Walsingham.

TURN LEFT AT GRANJA DE LA MORERUELA
- 700 miles - Seville to Santiago de Compostela, Spain. 1-903627 - 40 - 0 ....£14.95..
- 172 pages and 120 photographs

NORTH TO SANTIAGO DE COMPOSTELA VIA FATIMA -
1-903627- 44 - 3 - 650 miles from Lagos, Algarve, through Portugal via Fatima to Santiago de Compostela........£17.95.. - 220 pages and 160 photographs

ST. OLAV'S WAY - 400 MILES - NORWAY
- Photgraphic book and basic guide ...1 - 903627- 45 - 1 ....£12.95
- 124 pages and 130 photographs.

ST. WINEFRIDE'S WAY - 14 miles - St. Asaph to Holywell.
ISBN 1-903627-66-4   40 pages. 5 maps. 20 photographs..£6.95

ST. ALBAN'S WAY - 25 mile walk from Waltham Abbey to St. Alban's Cathedral.
Linking together two major medieval pilgrimage centres.
ISBN 978-0-9553691-3-1 48 Pages. 7 maps. 18 colour photographs. £7.95

ST. KENELM'S TRAIL by John Price - From the Clent Hills to Winchcombe Abbey - 60 miles. ISBN 978-0-9553691-6-2 . 60 pages 5 maps....£7.50

DERBYSHIRE PILGRIMAGES - The pilgrimage routes, saints and hermits of the county and Peak District. Plus a St. Bertram Walk and about a pilgrimage.
48 pages. £5.95

LONDON TO ST. ALBANS - 36 MILES ......NEW...... JSBN 978-0-9560649-7-4
80 pages. Wire bound. 45 photos. 8 maps. A stunning walk from Westminster to St. Albans via 32 churches. £9.95

FOLKESTONE, HYTHE TO CANTERBURY - 25 MILES ..NEW
ISBN 9780956064981..............68 pages. 40 colour phots. 8 maps. £9.95

LONDON TO CANTERBURY - 75 MILES.
ISBN 9780956064967 140 pages. 146 PHOTOS. 15 maps...................£12.95

LONDON TO WALSINGHAM - 190 MILES
ISBN 9780956464422...................256pages. 250 photos. 40 maps. ...£14.95

THE JOHN SCHORNE PEREGRINATION by Michael Mooney. 27 mile walk in Buckinghamshire to North Marston, the site of medieval miracles and pilgrimage.
A5. 56 pages. 16 colour photographs. 8 maps. £7.95
ISBN 978-0-9564644-0-8

ST CEDD'S PILGRIMAGE - 24 MILES - To St. Peter's Chapel on the Wall, near Bradwell on Sea. ISBN 978-0-9564644-7-7. 56 pages. A5 24 colour photos. 4 maps. £6.94

ST BIRINIUS PILGRIMAGE - 26 MILES - To his shrine in Dorchester Abbey, Oxfordshire.
ISBN 978-0-9564644-8-4 56 pages. 20 colour photos. 8 maps. £6.95

PILGRIM'S PASSPORT - ISBN 978-0-9568044-1-9 Specially designed book to record your sello's. £5.00

OUR LADY OF ULTING PILGRIMAGE WALK - 16 MILES - To a former Marian shrine is Essex, near Maldon. ISBN 978-0-9568044-5-7 £6.95

OUR LADY OF CAVERSHAM PILGRIMAGE WALK - 38 MILES - Windsor to Reading.
A5 wire bound. 80 pages. Maps and photos. £8.95 ISBN 978-0-9568044-6-4

MANDEVILLE MONKS WAY - 42 MILES - Edmonton Green (N. London) to Saffron Walden.
A5 Wire bound. 80 pages. Maps and photo's. £8.95. ISBN 978-0-9568044-7-1

THE ESSEX PRIORY WAY - 20 MILES - St. Osyth to Colchester, linking St. Osyth Priory and St. Botoloph's Priory together. Beautiful coastal walk. ISBN 978-0-9568044-8-8 £8.50

WALKING THE CAMINO DI ASSISI - 320 KM - My story of walking this route, following in the footsteps of St. Francis and his life story. A5. Wire bound 94 pages. 80 photos. £9.95
ISBN 978-0-9574186-2-2

AYLESFORD PILGRIMAGE - 13 miles from Rochester Cathedral to The Friars, Aylesford.

THREE SOUTH EASTERN PILGRIMAGES - Our Lady of Hartley, Kent; Wintershall Pilgrimage, Sussex and Our Lady of Consolation, Surrey.

see my website - **www.thejohnmerrillministry.co.uk**

Illustrated Talks
by Revd. John N. Merrill

John has countless talks on his recording breaking walks around the world.
For a full list contact John - Tel. 01992-762776
Email - marathonhiker@aol.com

His latest talks -

WALKING TO MONT ST. MICHEL - John has walked here twice - from Farnham via Winchester to Mont St. Michel (200 miles), and from Caen (100 miles) joining the annual pilgrimage walk organised by the Association of Chemins de Mont St. Michel. Both remarkable walks with the final 7km across the exposed sand, mud and rivers to the rock and abbey.

LONDON TO OXFORD PILGRIMAGE WALK - St. Frideswide Way - 93 miles. John discovers and traces the medieval pilgrimage route from Westminster Abbey to Christ Church Cathedral in Oxford, and the shrine of St. Frideswide. Then onto Binsey and her "forgotten" healing well; the Lourdes of the South.

WALKING ESSEX'S COASTLINE - 250 MILES - An exceptional walk around England's second largest county's coastline, rich in history, sea-birds and waders and more than 100 islands. A surprising journey.

WALKING MY WAY - The on going story of John's unique walking life, with some 219,000 miles walked. The stories and tales from his ground breaking walks around the world.

The Art of walking the John Merrill Way.

1. *Always set off in the clothes you plan to wear all day, given the weather conditions. Only on sudden changes in the weather will I stop and put on a waterproof or warmer clothing.*

2. *Set off at a steady comfortable pace, which you can maintain all day. You should end the walk as fresh as when you started.*

3. *Maintain your pace and don't stop. Stopping for any period of time disrupts your rythmn and takes upwards of a mile (20 mins) to settle back down into the flow/ease of movement.*

4. *Switch your phone off. Listen and enjoy the countryside - the smell of the flowers, bird song, the rustle of leaves and the tinkling stream, and observe the wildlife.*

5. *Ignore the mileage and ascents - don't tick the miles or hills, just concentrate on what the walk's goal is. To think otherwise slows you down and makes the walk a struggle rather than a joy. In a similar vein, when ascending just keep a steady pace and keep going. To stop is to disrupt the flow and make the ascent interminable.*

6. *Whist a walk is a challenge to complete, it is not just exercise. You should enjoy the world around you, the flowers, birds, wildlife and nature and look at and explore the historical buildings and churches that you pass. Industrial complex's have their own beauty. All are part of life's rich tapestry.*

7. *Remember that for every mile you walk, you extend your life by 21 minutes.*

8. *A journey of a 1,000 miles begins with a single step and a mile requires 2,000 strides.*

"The expert traveller leaves no footprints" Lao Tzu.

THE JOHN MERRILL FOUNDATION LONG DISTANCE WALKING CHARTER FOR THE UK.

1. All path signs to be made of wood and clearly state the right of way designation and destination, with correct mileage/kilometers. Individually designed, logo or symbols is to be encouraged. Variety and individuality is essential.

2. Wooden stiles are preferred to kissing gates. Kissing gates have a fatal flaw - many are not wide enough yo allow a backpacker with his pack to get in and out of without removing the pack. For half the year the central area is wet and muddy. The metal bar stiles with a wide base and narrow neck at thew top should be abolished; they are not suitable for backpackers - all have to take the rucksacks off to get through.
SOS - *Save our stiles* - part of our heritage.

3. All long distance routes to clearly state the start and end of the route on the ground, with an overall map showing the route at each end. Registration boxes at either end for signing in and out.

4. All long distance routes should provide regular places for wild camping. No ammenities required just a place to pitch a tent.

5. All temporary path closures should be notified from the nearest road and not at the start of a particular path - this results in having to walk back. The diversion or temporay alternative route should be clearly well signed.

6. Every walker should be trained to read a map, use a compass and calculate a gride reference. The dependence of modern technology is to be encouraged - but learn the basic skills.

7. All long distance walkers should wear well broken in and good fitting boots, wkith two pairs of socks, and carry the minumum basics in a suitable padded and framed rucksack.

8. All footpaths & rights of way's should be be regularly cleared of brambles, nettles, blow downs, and overhanging branches to allow a walker to pass through comfortably. Paths should be natural earth, not gravel, tarmac or rock slab.

9. Take your rubbish home - pack it in, pack it out.

10. Take only pictures.

11. Admire the flowers but do not pick them.

12. Say "hello" to all walkers that you pass.

13. Leave your headphones, music centre at home so you can enjoy the sounds of nature. Switch your phone off and only use in an emergency.

May the sun bring you new energy by day.
May the moon softly restore you by night.
May the rain wash away your worries.
May the breeze blow new strength into your being.
May you walk gbently through the world and
Know its beauty all the days of your life.

Apache blessing.

Look at the trees.
Look at the birds.
Look at the clouds.
Look at the stars ....
And if you have eyes
you will be able to see
that the whole of
existence is joyful.

Osho.

THE JOHN MERRILL MINISTRY
- a universal monk -
embracing & honouring
all faiths & none.

John has been following his own spiritual path all his life, and is guided. He was brought up as a Christian and confirmed at the age of 13. He then went to a Quaker Boarding School for five years and developed his love for the countryside and walking. He became fascinated with Tibet and whilst retaining his Christian roots, became immersed in Buddhism. For four years he studied at the Tara Buddhist Centre in Derbyshire. He progressed into Daoism and currently attends the Chinese Buddhist Temple (Pure Land Tradition) in London. With his thirst for knowledge and discovery he paid attention to other faiths and appreciated their values. Late in life he decided it was time to reveal his spiritual beliefs and practices and discovered the Interfaith Seminary.

'When the pupil is ready, the teacher will appear'. (Buddhist saying).

Here for two years he learnt in more depth the whole spectrum of faiths , including Jainism, Paganism, Mother Earth, Buddhism, Hinduism, Islam, Judaism, Sikhism, Celtic Worship and Shamanism. This is an ongoing exploration without end. He embraces all faiths, for all have a beauty of their own. All paths/faiths lead to one goal/truth. On July 17th. 2010 he was Ordained as a Multi-faith Minister.

*'May you go in peace, with joy in your heart
and may the divine be always at your side.'*

Using his knowledge and experience he combines many faiths into a simple, caring and devoted services, individually made for each specific occasion, with dignity and honour.
He conducts special Ceremonies -

Popular Funeral Celebrant and member of the Natural Death Society.

* Funerals * Memorial Services * Sermons * Weddings   *Civil Partnerships
* Baby Blessings & Naming
* Rites of Passage * Healing Ceremonies * Pilgimages * Inspirational Talks
Qigong Teacher.   Reiki Prationer.

For further information Contact John on -
Tel/Fax: 01992 - 762776   Mobile. 07910 889429
Email - marathonhiker@aol.com
Ministry site -www.thejohnmerrillministry.co.uk
All Faiths church - www.londoninterfaithchurch.co.uk

Revd. John N. Merrill, HonMUni
32, Holmesdale, Waltham Cross,
Hertfordshire EN8 8QY